Bestiary Dark

Also by Marianne Boruch

POETRY
The Anti-Grief
Eventually One Dreams the Real Thing
Cadaver, Speak
The Book of Hours
Grace. Fallen From
Ghost and Oar (chapbook)
Poems: New & Selected
A Stick that Breaks and Breaks
Moss Burning
Descendant
View from the Gazebo

PROSE ON POETRY
The Little Death of Self
In the Blue Pharmacy
Poetry's Old Air

MEMOIR
The Glimpse Traveler

Bestiary Dark

Marianne Boruch

Copper Canyon Press
Port Townsend, Washington

Cover art: Judith Nangala Crispin, *Four birds and a lizard return to their ancestors,
on spider-strings, over Mt Cooroora, in Kabi-Kabi Country.*
Five panel Lumachrome glass print, chemigram, cliche-verre. Landscape and sky:
cliche-verre and lumen from beached jellyfish, shed python skin, echidna spines,
spiders, human hair, garnia seeds, twigs, rainforest ochres, oil paint, vegemite,
petals and crystals made from copper chloride and acid with a current run
through it – with roadkill southern boobook owl, roadkill masked lapwing,
roadkill eastern water dragon, roadkill purple swamp hen, roadkill rainbow
lorikeet on fibre paper. Exposure times of between 29 and 41 hours under
acetate and perspex in humid conditions. Summer light and rain light.

Copper Canyon Press is in residence at Fort Worden State Park
in Port Townsend, Washington, under the auspices of Centrum.
Centrum is a gathering place for artists and creative thinkers from
around the world, students of all ages and backgrounds,
and audiences seeking extraordinary cultural enrichment.

LIBRARY OF CONGRESS CATALOGING-IN-PUBLICATION DATA
Names: Boruch, Marianne, 1950– author.
Title: Bestiary dark / Marianne Boruch.
Description: Port Townsend : Copper Canyon Press, 2021. | Summary:
    "Written following Marianne Boruch's 2019 Fulbright in Australia,
    and on the heels of the devastating fires that began after her departure,
    Bestiary Dark is filled with strange and sweet details, beauty, and impending
    doom—the drought, fires, and floods that have grown unspeakable in scale.
    These poems face the ancient, unsettling relationship of humans and the
    natural world—the looming effect we've wrought on wildlife—and what solace
    and repair our learning even a little might mean"—Provided by publisher.
Identifiers: LCCN 2021025521 | ISBN 9781556596377 (paperback)
Subjects: LCGFT: Poetry.
Classification: LCC PS3552.075645 B47 2021 | DDC 811/.54—dc23
LC record available at https://lccn.loc.gov/2021025521

9 8 7 6 5 4 3 2 1

COPPER CANYON PRESS
Post Office Box 271
Port Townsend, Washington 98368
www.coppercanyonpress.org

of the creatures, for them

—*Marianne, I thought you would like this article and it is better to send a short email than none at all.*

https://science.anu.edu.au/news-events/news/anu-gives-koalas-home-and-care-after-bushfires#:~:text=Koalas%20displaced%20and%20injured%20by,Australian%20National%20University%20(ANU)

I wanted to tell you Judith is safe and still fighting fires in her Hilux. We have a bad day today in Canberra, but are well prepared.

with affection,
Sarah

———————————

—In mathematics, the *epigraph* is the study of continuous real-valued functions. . . . For example, the position of a planet is a *function* of time.

A Prologue

The world, is it finite? began Pliny the Elder

on what he saw and heard, thirty-seven "books"

to round that up, first century CE as he

proceeded to be infinite. His *Naturalis.* His *Historia.*

Book VIII unto X: Land life and sea life, through-the-air

and underground life. Same as now.

Only *ancient*—the one thing

Pliny never imagined: he'd be ancient.

We watched the cassowary go famously

scary beside an ordinary house in Queensland,

a Tasmanian devil road-leap on cue at dusk,

Carmen on the radio west of Hobart, the Lyric Opera

all the way from Chicago to that end of the earth.

When you see a platypus love his mud

as he does, what happens?

Or while the echidna slips into grass as into a pocket.

And kangaroos, wallabies lying down to their

regal *so what* as brilliant birds

span out overhead without number.

You think this world doesn't know things? I asked the fires
from a distance. Did you think you can
do any damn thing you want?

Like asking a mad bad baby to fix cars or not eat
pablum or be a sweet polite cry in the night.

Contents, in the Manner of Pliny the Elder

BOOK TWO/ She of the Rescue Centre Answered

[xii]

BOOK THREE/ What Doesn't Define *Want?*

Bestiary Dark

BOOK ONE

I Could Redact Most Parts of Me So Memory

can't even reach them. I could, and really once
in Tasmania it was *you guys*

nearly off the map! our son wrote,
half mistaken-amazed as old cartographers in love
with vast, with a lot of water
around something, inking a three-headed dragon
to the corner.
Most didn't much leave their rooms.

Any *nearly*
equals beginning. Leave it to a map
to un-map. O cloud of close-your-eyes . . .

Hang on, said the sweet earnest boy
secretly writing his novel, selling us a printer
at Officeworks in Canberra
to over and over, the way

myth works any real story come along.

Real story: a fire about to be triggered
by ghost gums and lightning.

Or floods that overwhelm. Or such beautiful days.

I understand, I said to the Indigenous Elder.
No you don't, he said.

* * *

The quiet, the way a kangaroo
stops, stared at me, its little
T-rex arms frozen for how many minutes.

What I mean is—
                    I don't know what I mean.

In an elevator the body aches for gravity as that
smallest room of the house rises like
some weird high-handed helium's in charge of
armies and ships, childhood, history,
future's next day to next, major exports and imports
of whatever time, place, race, gender we get

jolts to a stop.

Look down while you're up there: alley and meadow,
the town dump crazy-winged with gulls,
minor royalty in the kingdom
of old mattresses, busted toys and shopping carts
no matter how inland.
But everywhere is inland when you know
how far the sea drops dark at
the edge of things.

Sea as idea, as Original Vague Rumor of Blue some
stranger had of water in the year of great fires.

Which year and whose year and how many years.

He walked away into
a little dot and spoke like a prophet.

I saw a mob of those dots
on the horizon most mornings—
kangaroos! joeys! more kangaroos!
I lifted my binoculars.

I see them too, big shot, an Archangel said in passing.

* * *

Fact is dreams come if you are tired enough
to say yes. I believed as a child.
Meaning I feared. Or I loved.
Or stood in the sun braced for those
stupid photos—Easter, Christmas, Fourth of July.

Redact, redact, erase, cross out, tear it up,
let the wind take it. And wind
showers down embers.

That's sleep, isn't it? So many
with arms crossing chest in perfect rehearsal
for the hit movie that might trade
this world for another.

It's that quiet. You think things.

My laptop screen has a tiny magnifying glass
leaning in the corner as if universe only
gets larger. Next to it
                    Tell me what you want to do.

Tell . . .
          who? I thought before falling.

* * *

Of course Pliny got here first with this bestiary thing—
world turned CE, two years pre-Pompeii, his
collecting, recollecting
every blur and fine point. It's how you watch birds
from a blind. You see and they don't,
the pond shrunk by drought.

Is the poem a telescope or a microscope?
Is it big to make small, or small to make big?
How much water in a poem divided by
        how much thirst? How much fire and ash?

A time machine can cherish or destroy.
And that rib toward a future,
                                    was it a fuse?

Orphaned wallaroo in my arms
a kind of baby kangaroo not really. One species here,
one species there. But they *resemble.*

At it, at it in that
slough of despond called *room,*
                        called *Rescue Centre.*
The little wallaroo I bottle-fed
filling the word *pensive* as stare, as
stop eating a moment—I see it, saw it, I did, I do—
surely his
        where is she

headlight-blinded at dusk, fooled by glare, crossing
for grass and a small welling up what once
was a pond, the driver—*Jesus! Where the hell?*—bent
for a shiny can rolling near the brake.

Bottle half the length of my hand
in my hand. His paws and giant legs
all akimbo in the flannel pouch.

His human eyes not quite fear but *warm* at that speed
meant milk mixed from a tin,
the bottle with its long tawny nipple, his mouth
frantic as any infant's for it.

* * *

What is a moment if not this:

      I   am   feeding   a joey   [stop]
   in   the   bush   capital   [stop]   *9,647 miles from home*

But a wallaroo in it! Low table, a couch, overstuffed
chair and chair high above the city. One window,
a door, four walls.
               I repeat: a wallaroo in it—

People said *lovely* so often it *was* lovely.
And *brilliant* half the time
to advance the cause of Yes and Okay, subspecies
of Pleasant. Or was it
             Phylum of Good Will,

Order of Forgive and Give Way,
Genus of Kindness or Grace or Smokescreen—

No Worries. No Worries. We'll get it sorted.

Stories got told: *I took one to work, tucked in this,*
this shirt. The big meeting went on, that dodgy invoice
they talked into the ground but I
could feel him right there . . .

Vague rumor of blue,
a prophet who walks into *desolate,* into a dot.

A paw to his face like a cat, tidying up. Then curled as a leaf,
a wallaroo in my arms sated as far back
as milk is, as sleep is.
          Historia Naturalis, according to Pliny.

* * *

Not exactly what Dante thought—
his "hopeless, pathless, lightless woods forgot."
I mean by dawn pre-fire and flood,
gum trees in their striptease
down to bare yellowish skin that took sunlight cold
like you starve a fever. Until I almost believed

the planet clear-eyed enough to make
its southern claim: autumn in May!
Season wildly misplaced,
its leaves gold or red when they
should be back to buds, a beginning, a rabble-rousing.
Spring, for Christ's sake! I got so mixed up.

Poetry = a tree Dante hollowed out and stepped inside to wait.

Pliny's first measure. The Roman world
hoarded up, full

> Of *venomous and poisonfull honey*
> Of *the glo-worms*
> Of *the Smell of good ground*
> Of *Wolves,* Of *Dogges,* Of *Swine*
>   *and their natures*

Wet things surely recounted no matter how I mis-imagine.

But you must *un-imagine,* sang the Archangel from trees,
Pliny's real

> *Dolphins, Sperm and Killer Whales,*
>   *purple fishes—*
> his *many-foot fish, sea-nettle fishes, other*
>   *nastie and filthie creatures*

caught, kept for real in the middle of his brain, 77 CE.
Hell of a guy with eyes and ears
in that boat at Pompeii.

> That Pliny, too bad about dying as

the land spewed fire, the Archangel crooned
old-school, like Sinatra.

* * *

History: a whodunit, a lie, a prayer, a questionnaire.

1) Did fish dive deeper at Pompeii, its mountain imploding?
2) Does close looking change any first or final thing?
3) What does ache itself ache for?

(You, said the Elder first week, what makes you think you
can write about our animals?)

In fact, Pliny's boat sinking sideways
with his weight, what he knew inside the load he wrought was

         everything + all of it so far

as he was able, as long as he was able—

Desperate steaming harbor where
fumes went lethal. He breathed *in* all right. No, I don't
picture it quiet.
         But water *should* be soothing,
         boats *should* make it okay

to the other side, even in rain
lit as lightning. All those *shoulds,*

     like that great bushfire in Canberra years ago

should have taken out every huge eucalyptus: did
and did not, so many charred lower trunks we saw, the gutted
could-be-but-aren't just stumps.
         I looked up.
Leaves still sprang off new branches—
a trick, a WHAAAAAT!?—
To come back from the dead. A how-in-the-world?
is hope. Of a sort. *Of a sort . . .*

Really? How many lives are we given, how much
happenstance in us? What the hell *time* is it?

Ask the platypus. Ask that patchwork of creature
that can't keep its species straight.

[12]

The Archangel shrugged, *Look at me! I'm part bird too!*
My wings wing out like a god-given
cockatoo's, note my spiky
yellow crest up there—more sulfur-esque by the minute,
best yellow ever . . .
      Cheeky hybrid wannabe

taking a glorious bird's name in vain,
all celestial-glow about it.

* * *

True, the Archangel's voice—almost the same
as the cockatoo's shriek, flight-wise and leaf-sick,
a tree-to-tree that shatters.
Like its cousin's too,
                    red-tailed and black—

"the flying bolt-cutter"—John the Bird Whisperer
spotted it gnawing through a branch.
John who walked with us, showed us secret places of
feather and burrow, river and rock.

Or was that archangel's pitch and moan
the Australian raven's unheavenly *ca* and *ca,*
its beaten child's
caaaaaa trailing off to
little bone-piles of nothing—

Those (*hopeless, lightless, pathless*) nights the old
go their last, done-in, the final
sliver of knowing anything on Earth is
erase erase. Just another death.

So tracks an archangel's eye from great heights.

That terrible *caaaa*
downslurring from trees or streets narrowed by
every car's slow distracted start.

Eating supper by the window we thought
a real child out there.
We thought to call someone.

* * *

Is the Past what's left in the glove compartment
of a totaled car? Disc five there once,
the library lectures-on-tape (*Daily Life in the Ancient World*)
however fog-socked-in shattered day of arrival.

But *arrival:* that would be

the Present waiting for a Future to soothe
and clean up after spills, the bloody broken moving parts.

What a mess. Poetry. Just a lot of questions
answered the dumb way, the muddy hard way
via the silence it comes from,

the mirror that reverses and breaks when you stare into it,
the camera that won't click right anymore.

Be careful what you predict, poet,

what you hang on to
like a prophet does. Be careful of
that ever-distant dot on the horizon in you
as you walk into fire and flood.

* * *

Sometimes I wrote things down: *when land*
parts for a ferry in Brisbane, fish know
it's been rain of a morning,
and wind. At times I took dictation—
their underwater radar of *Dart, don't dart,*
of *Beware all that lies above*
though below the bottom creepers have their own
wilderness and fierce jaws.

If ever I know anything, one foot then
another lifted and put down, traveling by way of
bones in me, bones
packed with blood and nerve and a dash
of muscle, nothing will allow me
the brilliant side-eye of any fish miraging past rocks
and broken machines heaved into water,
hated chairs, old wallpaper, bills unpaid, a letter
with its recent bad news said so well, a dismal
wad of charm still dissolving.

Fish swam by, a straightforward mystery
dividing oxygen from hydrogen,
gills opening and closing like blinds in a window
you can't quite figure how that
tangle of string works, as in *murky* as in
lower, as in *region.*

Look from the ferry, bow and stern
part and small parcel of any of us born to
tragedy, the day down there,
lots of blue *regardless* going on.

* * *

Dear Thus and So. Dear Eventually

all of us lose the gene *could,* trading it off
for *can't* and *sleep alone* like
the pelican in the vast reserve lost his
long-term mate to bored ducks in a bad mood
marauding in Pond Four. Their revenge for
who-knows-what, just to wear her out.
Or it was fun. Or it was time.
Called Mildred, and too old. She got tired.

A detail about him: one wing gone,
after and also.

So he's stuck there solo in paradise, given
a human name too—*George*—
in dubious compensation.
A king reigning over waterfowl with a history.

What I could not see—but did—
was another pelican, one on Dairy Road
dipping down to
swallow a whole fish whole.

Noon glare, long pinkish throat lit up—
to x-ray! Live shadow-shape
ricocheted in there, down.

Bestiary of mind, unnerve, unnerve . . .

* * *

Friends, stop. This happened, I swear,

before terrible fires impressed
    their little Pentecostal tongues of flame
    all over the internet map like
    a holy card hallucinates,

before both the brave and the timid wore
    gas masks to bed.

Friends, this was *pre*-fire, *pre*-knitting of mittens
    for dazed burnt koalas,

before poets began watering the bees,
before the floods finally came,
before present turned past to reconfigure a future.

Medieval enough, going dark, this nowhere-else
all of them: platypus, koala, emu on the run,
echidna spiked as grass that lies back
in wind or rain, steady multiple kangaroos
and wallabies upright or lying
sideways as if at a company picnic downing
martinis in the grassy expanse.

We hiked to see the rock paintings. We sat
for a while, a few yards
from some roos in the shadow of
their afternoon. An old female
pressed forward on those little arms to rise,
to try to rise.

We—full speed ho-hum to them, so nothing at all
in the next patch of gum trees.
Solidarity, sister! She
was me and we
were us—bad joints need oil, cross species—
as she hitched herself up.

Recollect is to rescue,
      to invite back the plain astonishments.

That's the dream, to get away, is it not? *We'll sit, we'll*
walk happily to find the rock wall they painted
a thousand years back, to go back . . .

Open your book, Pliny, still *at it at it* as if
that raised roar of earth at Pompeii didn't keep raging,
as if fires in Australia skipped the loved places.

BOOK TWO

She of the Rescue Centre Answered

first thing—
Someone is poisoning magpies. *Keep the bodies*
out of the freezer. We'll study their livers.

People suck! she said, hanging up. But the Indigenous Elder
could have told me that.

On the wall, a poster. Bogong moths roosting in vacant caves,
loving the cool air. Migrations go haywire in drought.

Another call: someone's hit a roo.
The joey's sweet but going crazy on the sunporch.
This afternoon, okay. We'll come by.

She still could be shaking her head. *Bloody drivers.*
It's the glare, she thinks aloud. *They could not see to see.*

Dickinson wrote nearly exactly that to
nail down a last moment, just after her *And then*
the windows failed— I can't tell cause from effect,
one overlay from another.

As for the magpies, their livers surely tried to clear, to strain
the poison. Fast or slow, the birds, I bet—
—how many?—flew just fine for a while in screechy loops.
Then to fall, to try up again. And failing.

Shiny black/white feathers run aground near the roses . . .

Most raucous caroling in the garden, silent for once.

Is that what alerted the caller? Behind the house,
a sudden. It was vast.

* * *

After tai chi where the hand's called
wing with new powers, talk over coffee
and sandwiches turned to bees, twice! I blurred

to three-quarter time until a digital insect rave
in my head kicked up like a fire that ravishes is said
to sound, a train or jet gearing up but muted,

quiet that close, those hives of males
doing nothing but do it, do it, O Queen
while female *worker* bees glory in their travels,

their own rising octave bearing down
on rose and marigold and sage.
Herself back at the box, long-lived,

imperial, larger than a dime, she auto-loves
and loves, her million-lens eye
on the future of the charges she discharges.

Before my wing turned back to mere hand on a key
or quite frozen because I slept funny, every bee
we spoke of—I swear!—had my wing, a whirl,

an abstraction of wing if I could pencil it, pen,
crayon cobalt—the bluest! Still. Poor males
die doing it. Boom, it's over. Then they're over.

Coffee too. And the jagged last half of sandwich.
Even chocolate, more spiritual quest than a taste
at that table, brief semisweet of another life.

* * *

Pond Four, on rerun: Ranger Kaz
sings out *Musk Duck*
Musk Duck—
                    his father was an egg!

That duck swims close and looks at her.
Fondly? Yes. Absolutely fondly.
She calls him "Ripper."

(I still laugh at that. And hold it close.)

Then there's the teen platypus in the world
not secret this time, all not-nocturnal afternoon out
of the burrow practicing his
prison break, little delinquent. He *should*
wait like the others until dark
to nuzzle swamp reeds, nubs, passages,
to lightning-prod muddy spots, to
dive the shallows seventy-two times
each hour. That's seventy-two
times an hour
                into the old cheek-pouch.

Young Platypus, your duck bill
hotwired! You of
                the Sacred Order of

the Electric Jaw That Knows a Tasty Bite or Two.

* * *

*Again The Walk: Once you reach the carpark at Namadgi National Park,
you will see a large sign that provides information about the Yankee Hat
Aboriginal Art Site. Beyond the sign, the start of the walking track is very
inviting, with open plains and wetlands shadowed majestically by the
nearby mountain of Yankee Hat and a little farther to the south-west Mt
Gudgenby (image 2). The total distance of the walk is just over six kilome-
tres return, so it's not arduous and very suitable for families.*

1. Thus you *commence* the walk. Thus a *first footbridge* crossing
   Bogong Creek.

2. OMG, the native welcome swallows swoop for insects, second
   on their to-do list of a morning, the peace of mind/no-mind no
   human gets.

3. If they do stop (rarely) you see their colors (blue   white   rufous).
   But prose into poetry is cutthroat-brief.

Dragonflies, grassland, wooded *enclaves* before the mountain where
trees darkened us with their friendship.

It's Rudy, the snake guy: If you ever
roll a log, turn it inward, so it's *away* where the red-bellied
black snake sleeps under.

I watch how he does that. I watch sun invade a solitude.

But everything slept under.
Kilometres, not miles. Metres, not yards
below masked lapwings and the wedgetail
so fiercely an eagle, always on updraft.

They painted a human without a spear, a roo midleap,
a dingo, a turtle, an emu on that rock we walked to.

> *Come hither, beloveds. Celebrate!*—800, maybe
> 1200 years of ochre and clay for red and yellow,
> charcoal for black and what binds color
> to stone is sap or blood or both.

Once-a-year bogong moths

in migration, a sweet fat,
a dissolve in the mouths of those who first
gathered in that spot moving

in and out of the poem.

* * *

Even before the Great Burning
what of endangered koalas sleeping through it all
in eucalyptus trees, in this Sanctuary
therefore *sanctified*.
                Koalas stink, oh, and in drought!

a New Zealander flat-out told me (can you trust a Kiwi
in Australia, an Aussie in New Zealand?)
Too little water up through roots into leaves which is

all they eat or drink. Worse, consider
the fires burning to ash one-metre-down microbes
that should offer all things to those koalas
straight out of earth via trees—
so the forester held forth.
                If Indigenous

(he was not), he'd say *Country*
like it's the beginning of time, like it's a *thing*.

Even you—YOU—could come back as dirt,
the Elder told me. Even you could get lucky.

A most triumphant reverent re-up—dirt!—
all-giving link in the chain.

Koalas are cute, the Archangel said,
but their dreams scare me.

Merely human, I ran out of neck to bend back, tops of trees
lost in that eucalyptus grove.
Just once I spotted a koala high in—was it?—
a scribble gum.

Still, who was I to those giants? Couldn't gauge
how distant that leafing out was.
To know something though, a furry
small something, his back
to me, his ass to me, to be sweetly exact.

To *see* other life living

                this life . . .

As for the scribble gum, its name
means larvae encrypting a feeding trail between
old bark and new, raised marks as
brilliant as Braille.

             I mean to say, writes

the tiniest not-yet-moth,

                want out want out want out—

* * *

Meanwhile the name—*koala*—means in what tongue,
whose mouth and DNA, through how many eons?

Poetry, ditto. Buried business of the body, DNA back
to seas parting, continents shifting, how
long it's been and what's to come.

(Weren't the fires listening, just waiting at that point?)

Ko-al-a! Look it up, idiot, the Archangel roused me.
What do you
mortal hybrids say now? *Google it—*

                                you bone & flesher,
part shiny-metal-jointer
in failed sockets, reckless bias-machine from
your too-little-time to know anything, brain dissolving
with getting older. What's age to me?—a hybrid
eons before Uluru got to be Uluru,
before scat began telling the likes of you things like
who is who out all night
scrounging food though in fact
that's private, that's none of your beeswax!

I nodded to the tiny mites feasting
in his gorgeous hair as he
walked away. Classic archangel braggadocio!

I did look it up: *koala,* an Indigenous word for *no water.*
There they were, up in trees eating only leaves.

Koala scary dream #7: fur on fire.

* * *

All night I slept through lives. Lives of boney saints
flung out prostrate, going up in flames, or years
atop poles in the desert. Lives of
kangaroos staggered by headlights, stepping into roads
that will orphan their joeys. Snakes
fiercely harmless in the bush, but I recoiled, stepped back . . .

I slept through lives of cheap nonsense, alert to
the buying and selling, to what's on sale
at the mall. Or partway through sleep, getting up
in whatever dim room—a full bladder the thing
I forgot would turn up in my kit, what I
did not leave back at the fort, reluctant step by step
to that *must* as demanding as a military raid
I never wanted in on
or to witness, the body's aching unlit.

Half-life of urgency and worry and in-between and shrug.

The wombat burrows his five-star tunnel
near the river. And gets flooded out in any hard rain,
year after year not learning.
No move to higher ground. All night my
quandary, my animal claims me.

* * *

A huge loop-de-loop in the blue: what *is* that?

We fixed binoculars on it.
John the Bird Whisperer's two zero-in guesses—
the black kite's helicopter spin, or swoop

of eagle, a wedgetail obsessed with high mysteries.

Who brought the strongest lens, the steadiest hold,
that cloudless morning in Canberra?

Still autumn at that point, going into winter. Post-fire
and pre-fire. A planet glorious,
upside down and inside out and we

glad amateurs who tracked it.

Who among the three of us spots the real thing first?
Just a plastic bag wind-socked, whirled, signaling
from the heavens. No bird at all!

Too many ways to think this hilarious-strange.

We never parse right what is comic,
what is tragic. Strewn gifts of the sea

pile up, trash once cups, straws, stray tackle,
a mini-sick cornucopia swallowed by
fish and seabirds cut open
for the grimmest museum display.

Sea turtles splayed there too behind glass to show
of course, of course—

down the hatch, you flimsy filmy bags from
Produce, swimming aloft and under, mistaken
for jellyfish those turtles love.

* * *

Some new-century Pliny bent over a map reconvenes
human knowledge with a gavel,
remeasures the shrinking bestiary: birds, this percent gone,
mammals, that percent and still subtracting, flames
or no flames.

Books rot in the stacks.
                    Who listens to the dead?

Just wind and dust and lost creatures now: the Tasmanian tiger
and dusky flying fox, the rufous bristlebird,
Gould's mouse and so on and on and more, the world's sleep
dark dreams
                    smoke smoke smoke
                    fire fire fire
                    water water no water

Add the Threatened, add the No-Longer-Rivers,
add *it's blood all over the earth out there.*
Add music, whose main bony structures
are pause and repeat.

Like Chaplin in the old movie
orders one bean for cheap, napkin at his throat,
cutting in half, in fourths, in eighths
the one bean given,
eternal graying afternoon through the café window.

Add "and yet—"
                    Saddest phrase in English, it's been
told and retold
and I've said on repeat as if

language begins in regret
and a warning, last thing in the world,
simple bean on a plate.

What a good trick, present and past and future
triple-ghosting the moment.

Those kangaroos full-face or profiled
once a ten-minute walk from our door in Canberra
on the verge of
                  stare back,

on the cusp of their no fear at all, their
so? how many lifetimes—

* * *

So we get there just as
some asshole—forgive me—on a joyride in
the outback runs her down, the emu,
and keeps going. After all, he's
got a planet to desecrate.

A very long line of
feathered-bloody-something, she's lifting now

and falling back to the road, not exactly
an ostrich but as lordly, and slower each time.

Don't fool yourself. It wasn't wind, not
a broken hinge crying out to open a door.

Our worthless offerings—

O Emu, here's our numb speechlessness.
But there are those who drive to
who-cares-if-I-kill and never regret. We *willed*
that news to her
medieval as prayer, all abruptly
stricken in the Flinders,

the handwringing two of us as

another acolyte stepped from his truck with a huge
plumber's wrench to bash her kindly
a good

one two three—

her *ooaa* each time faint, fainter
ooaa on a loop, a loop . . .

Reader, you who think poems
should never *story* too much or render
news of the day,

I need to get this right—

grief is human-speak for *emu*.
Night's quiet since then.

BOOK THREE

What Doesn't Define *Want*?

The spider's hope for the saw-toothed circle
she reels out, those spit threads she
wheedles straight: wind billows
but does not break.

How much sunlight loves a window too.
How much the garden does not care how much it grows
weary of growing. All night the moon hangs
its melodrama there.

He lies under a bed, old cat
too old to recognize mouse or
moth lost to wool.
He hides from a crack of thunder where

the sound of that, the sound
of that, insistent.
Sudden something in woods at night.
Abrupt, you turn like prey.

In the Reserve, I cleavered down hard
to bite-size the carrots, silverbeets, sweet potatoes for
wallabies endangered, fed in
"The Sanctuary"—ie: a sacred place.

I earned a blood blister for my trouble.

Every time I looked at my hand—
Every time.   I look.   At my hand.

* * *

The art historian told me a fish, on command, produced
a coin in the fresco. Saint Peter walks over

to plead for the temple tax all twelve of them needed
plus the one who urged him to talk to the fish

in the first place. So I saw that radiant creature
half out of the river, mouth open, the coin not nearly

as lit as the fish got to be. The paint those days
copied sunlight exact. Apparently what I missed

in catechism for as lapsed as I am—*fallen away*—
I'd remember if told the Renaissance

recorded and framed such a story. People imagine anything.
But truth too can be quirky. Four centuries later

some thought the platypus fake, dim England's brightest
certain the bill sewed on, the pouch a clever addition,

and fur—on this weirdling with duck feet? As for the fish
and its coin, a painted saint in clear supplication, not

by a long shot a Dreamtime story, I'd admit to
the Indigenous Elder, nothing next to

how that enormous rainbow Snake loosened its coil
to lie down and make a river. Or the Songlines,

the Ancients chanting into the real thing each valley
and mountain as they walked the length of a continent.

Well, you take what origin you get. But surely it *means*—
my delight in how a man is bent to a fish in gratitude,

the fish doing its selfless job *to get the show on the road*
my mother's raised eyebrows might have said. The way

I first looked at a platypus, his dive into mud and gloom—
charmed! And so signaled her ghost.

* * *

The pelican minus a wing must still
be Pelican George in Pond Four drying out
in sun or shadow what feathers remain, just like

before the fire when they moved him to the weir
until the world came back.

He's eyeing the ducks that did in his mate, his Mildred.
Where *is* she, where . . . ?

Surely he keeps looking.
Because brain-locked in him must be the worst.
Because in fact he too fell to the task,

that toxic buzz the time those ducks ganged up
and got her good. To be one of them, oh one of them!

Yay-to-Be-Mindless, most thrilling confusion.
(Might as well be human, the Archangel laughed.)

Maybe that pelican knew us. He looked across water.
In a blink, the world regrets its old story
to make a new story.

(Ancient Pliny's shrug on this afterlife thing: *As if ghosts
sequestered from the body have sense.*)

Says the ranger in my dream of her—*George!
Kaz here, I get it,*
walking toward him, *we all have damaging
multiple worlds in us.*

He looks away: *I did no wrong* he must think of

the shade now, in my dream. And when I wake
in full daylight his one wing up,
making that shade.

* * *

The taxidermist in the revered museum
stares down head and claw on the table to make

something whole again. Perhaps she's unnerved
by the prospect, death back to life. That we crave

not just *intact* but *true* is the first wish as when
an old mount from the '30s is taken out of

the standard formal pose of that day, its
upright-for-eternity habit of ninety years,

a straight-ahead looking through glass.
Lie down, the taxidermist might soothe

that forever young red kangaroo, trading bone
for wire to make the old arsenic-laced stuffing

release and relax into our mode and our fashion
or foam-replace its skeleton completely

before she needles up the time-stopped creature
that will slip to the ground to lounge

confident and casual in pretend desolation,
some outback diorama I would have loved

every Saturday had I been a child in that city.
Surely I *was* a child in that city, surely prophecies

reverse and reclaim—so much life to redo.
Finally that manta ray in her workshop.

We stood staring into the freezer, cold clouds
rising up. *Washed up on shore, pregnant, twin*

females in utero, is what the taxidermist told me.
Cheers for scalpel and patience. *Cheers all around then,*

she said, *like a delivery room in here!* Like a real
break-out-the-wine, I thought, like confetti.

* * *

Trees lined the road
into the outback, the usual
eucalyptus jerked every which way
winter ache does, huge branches
dropping bark, crooked strips as if
the night before
a drug war, a fight, a drunken frenzy.

All of it to the ground.

Beyond the paddocks the quarrels
of a few small birds. Not even cockatoos
hung around in their noisy usual.

Tell me, I'd look grand
as a cockatoo, right?

That was the Archangel in my ear, ad nauseam.
Want is want, whatever feathered shape it is.

At the rest stop someone left a measured
pile of stones, a meaning.

* * *

A tiny pre-kangaroo slips out its mother's

low sweet spot, blind as certain insects to follow
the spit road she tongued down her belly
for this bit of pre-stars and vapor,

pre-meteor whatnot inch-worming up that line
of seasick wet, pioneering what's possible
toward the pouch to be a pinkie then months to

fur-out there past flood and drought and fire
unto big or really big, a gray or a red,
matter-of-fact leaping marvel of the bush.

Over coffee on a clear cold afternoon, the scientist
thirty years astonished at this route
that would never make it fully fleshed to MapQuest.

The Great Salt Road, the Great Silk Road,
nameless multiple Alpha/Omega Great Roads of
Blood and Pillage and Threat

and Greed—the human movie glitters
its awful special effects. What to make
of this world's greatest, *The Great Spit Road,*

warm wool bent back, narrow shiny and soak.

What do you think?

OUR MISSION:

Poetry is vital to language and living. Copper Canyon Press publishes extraordinary poetry from around the world to engage the imaginations and intellects of readers.

Thank you for your thoughts!

BOOK TITLE: _____

COMMENTS: _____

_____

_____

Can we quote you? ☐ yes ☐ no

☐ Please send me a catalog full of poems and email news on forthcoming titles, readings, and poetry events.

☐ Please send me information on becoming a patron of Copper Canyon Press.

NAME: _____

ADDRESS: _____

CITY: _____ STATE: _____ ZIP: _____

EMAIL: _____

 Copper Canyon Press

A nonprofit publisher dedicated to poetry

MAIL THIS CARD, SHARE YOUR COMMENTS ON FACEBOOK OR TWITTER, OR EMAIL POETRY@COPPERCANYONPRESS.ORG

CopperCanyonPress.org

BUSINESS REPLY MAIL
FIRST-CLASS MAIL   PERMIT NO. 43   PORT TOWNSEND WA

POSTAGE WILL BE PAID BY ADDRESSEE

Copper Canyon Press
PO Box 271
Port Townsend, WA 98368-9931

* * *

This   is   crazy

dot/dashed into mantra
    the abandoned telegraph way, sand for decades
    claiming the first station

that ghosted code and voice, lost urgencies in that
    drift between States, *States of Being* like
    South Australia, Western Australia, dreaded
    Nullarbor Plain threading one to the other near
    the bluest bight, our plan to wander—
    And risk water and life out there? They said no,

    do not, do not!

Of course, cautions went legend: few decent wells,
    scarce gasoline in the outback, no fully
    sealed roads, UFOs hovering in wait, thieving
    would-be murderers in dust and low growth
    fake-begging rides.

Oh yes, we were warned at suppers and carparks,
    in hallways, on trails, even my drawing group
    spoke up, sweetest art center in Belconnen
    where we worried our parking out front illegal.

But this new word to me. *Tablelands* in Canberra
    meant: stay. All those warnings = stay with us.

Land as *table,* as if you could sit down forever,
    pure evening solace of
    plate, a cup warm or cool to the brim is how
    I first loved that word before
    knowing what, if anything, of altitude.

No one says *down under* there.

* * *

Emu, you woke up?

I did. I did. Or I do. Or I am. Or I almost.

What about those two hand-wringers who
dragged you off the road?

The Americans?
I heard the numb knot in their heads trying to untie itself.

Emu! What about that killer-savior
of the heaviest wrench
stopping his truck,
smashing you to grit and god-forsaken
once twice three times to his
I'm sorry, I'm sorry . . .

That bastard of love.
My inner eyelid, the second one that opens sideways—
I lay there and saw what I saw.

And the murderous driver?

All exhaust and cutthroat fumes be his.

Where are you now, Emu?

Exactly where you are. In the italics.

* * *

Cows. They have stupid eyes, friend so dear

to me wrote. But I'd bring her back to see sheep
in the paddock step out of their fleece
like the gleaming bodies she knew from the bath,

washing child after child those years.
She'd like that. Poet. Painter. Silenced
by cells gone ruthless, not telling one of us.
 I can't hold that against her.

The stricken body gets so familiar it turns
to a rag. It must be hung on a line to dry. I'd tell her
I know now what's solitary. And what isn't.

Sheep, their abrupt nakedness inside that fence wasn't

a simple matter, blade and blood, radiant fold
on fold distant under one giant eucalyptus
for shade, bare bodies by way of the shearing

a shock. Nor the Old Masters, what they did

never easy either. To brush in a backdrop, burnt umber
and bone black warming up each
room in their paintings, laying down sorrow

as context, as drapes that part only at
the most beloved lit whatever-it-is, what she left.

* * *

So you're remembering sheep now too, the Archangel
came into my dream last night to bug me.
Do-mes-ti-cated creatures gone wild?

What's it to you? I cheeky'd back.

All the roaming feral ones: cattle, goats, brumbies.
Intrusives too? Like rabbits rabbits rabbits?

No. No camels either, I said, nope,
never spotted a single camel or rabbit out there. But every
each of what I saw slowed,
stick-skinny sleepwalkers crossing roads out of habit to water
as if a small blue
waited suspended in drought whether
real or not.

Dry as a bone, these rivers, we clichéd together
and drank our swill like the old men we'd never be
sit around repeating themselves.

The River Dust unto Dust, The River Need Not Apply,
River-No-Rain-for-Eight-Months-and-Counting.

Every outback spot you look, a once-river, an un-river.

I'm reading a book on this, I blurted out to the Elder.

Sure you are, he said.

I told him: See the boxes I checked?

[x] Pretty Much Agree.

[x] Most Sick-at-Heart Agree.

BOOK FOUR

IT'S LIKE THIS I TOLD THE ARCHANGEL

who can't swim—

crazy crowded under great waters

two hours from shore so misleading a dull vast gray

(not even blue if you look from the boat)

a full nothing really except you could say notable ships

(with questionable if not)

despicable captains dissolved a century and decades ago

(also the unfamous lost to)

who knows where plus storms

(of course storms)

a terrible reverie kicks in wind the stopped motor as they

laid out tea little cups of little cakes the earnest

(young marine biologists charts and maps)

the possible end of it all be careful heating more

(and more down there)

month after month roiling therefore queasy but instantly

(as one goggles up drops and snorkels in)

OMG! EVERYONE HERE! ALL ALONG! IN FULL COLOR!

lucky the boat found suspended over

(down and down)

clownfish orange and white gobies' tiny blazing yellow

the thick-lipped speckled wrasse damselfish triggerfish

(blue as the deepest bruise)

there's a movie black and white to sudden every color

(you know it   you do)

you grew up with it   as if longing is belonging   she closes

her eyes   she recites   like a schoolgirl   her anti-panic device

(set to go off)

even now, this century   there's no place like . . .   out of straw

(a brain then   an echoing)

emptiness morphs   to a heart   fear   to a great fear remembered

(thus muffled by)

a gleaming medal = courage   Christ   so much is hard   hard

to believe   it gets harder   the simple point

(great waters of the reef   go silent)

when there's bad news   coral fewer and fewer   but

(it's fine   a sign)

triumphantly ordinary-fine when   creatures still noise-up

(click and whine and crack open and shut)

in such a spot we fanned out   our drift   and drag

(how and why   skimming)

mountains   valleys deeper than lost fabled cities   hundreds

(all manner   thousands)

graceful creatures   finned   clawed and aglow   unimagining

who they are

(no thanks to our dead language names for them)

a curtain   pulled back   to   their just here thing

beloved certain neighborhoods over time   relished-remembered

(a real racket down there   eating   mating   fighting)

forgetting where they put their glasses and keys—

       (See? You are paying attention!)

how tiniest fish   for a home in the reef   need to listen

        (they listen   to swim-find that hidey-hole)

so much still   gorgeous   except places of die-off

       (quiet grayout   too warm)

for-the-waving-brilliant-living   all of them   we swimmers

          (mere shadows   falling)

part of   that dark that keeps dropping

I learned to read any   color as light   I told the Archangel

        (who didn't buy that either)

light as schools of moving light   every corner

         (we turned)

such blues   and yellows   dappled   striped   though

      (that yes and yes)

              no corners

* * *

A kangaroo in flight
or bent forward, set to spring off bark
some poet cut, flattened out, and began to paint
a century ago the Indigenous way, this straight-up interplanetary
anatomy lesson: elusive sphere of belly clearly in there,
skinny star routes linked up and down the body's
galactic interior, small planets blue
and green for brain, heart, then the big clanging bent legs
jet-streamed at the ready, those
little dino arms that could clip bloody anything
or chuck a wee joey to a pouch, once-moving parts frozen
in the painting as if laid bare
by the first oldest x-ray for the ever-after black endless
in profile: how I might dream if I were
half roo myself in release and let go of my
human-haves-and-never-had-really,
better thrown to graveyards I whistle past,
why not, and leap—

* * *

Don't worry about what goes on in the canopy, we don't,
insisted the Elder when I said *What?*

(That was me, *whatting* all over the place.)

Spirits live there untold, he said, untelling. It's earth
and under we care about. That's Country.

Earth is sentient—is how the Indigenous artist put it.

Meanwhile, the canopy? Not exactly a shrug, more a
we are not permitted.

Not permitted, a slow
freedom: you can't decide all things where
insects kingdom-off and over,
where tiny birds go high, in secret, a luscious
yellow-green flash, another and another . . .

Make the brain a patch of fertile ground, he
must have meant, *look up from there.*

* * *

The lyrebird, hidden. His dance, hidden. His wish to dance also
hidden. But he will get the girl.

His featherless, out of the egg pre-wish to dance hidden too.

His *hidden* hidden. His pre-egg in the nest, hidden. Its yolk and white
not yet yolk and white, equally hidden.

A song the lyrebird steps to and into. By heart and habit.
But hidden. Ditto that wild footloose, the very thing
also hidden from us, the thing famous and forlorn and ecstatic.

His mimic song, an old sound-effect record from the '50s, a camera's
click then its whirl, a braking truck, car alarm, chainsaw

plus twenty other birds screaming. Properly: *redoes* them.
His sound bites, more worldly the better
to woo-wow her. Under trees. On the little mound he's cleared

to dance. The way ahead circled by thorns and, higher up, stars.

How small must one be
to be hidden? How large to pass through larger things hidden—
sky by clouds, rain by darkness or dawn,
hopelessness by the wish for what's next and next.

Please. Don't think fire, not yet. Or smoke, flight, the dark all day
a kind of pandemic. Too early or too late in those woods.

But we saw a posted alert for the *is:* this bird can dance
and sing his way into that mythic throb
of lady-business. Some resourceful someone

made it precise and only slightly pornographic the arrow (this way!)
to where he-of-the-one-track-mind might stand and hide

in the voice of such worldly things.

The wooden notice nearly sang what he's up to, the bird's dance and song, his fabulous hind feathers to hypnotize the very one who maybe thought all along she'd have some other fate.

Hidden but about to *not* be, hidden but ancient unto the day.

No, we never saw him. Or her, for that matter. But me, a life member, the World Congress of the Disappointed, I understand hope.

As in, who knew art was involved? It's a sign.

* * *

Every available blue for no reason the sky is because the bower-
bird's meticulous in love. (*Another sex-u-al in-ter-lude,* my old teacher
intoned years ago in a class on Tennessee Williams, and we loved
that, we'd go crazy.) So the bowerbird keeps thieving, rearranging for
his starry moment in the picnic grove

   —a shattered blue ballpoint
   —crumpled napkins, all purple
   —a sample-size bottle of blue something
   —blue feathers (maybe a fairy wren or a kingfisher off course)
   —a child's pacifier, a blue sneaker charm from a bracelet
   —torn bits of the bluest blue wings still shimmering as leaves
        above throw light like the ventriloquist's voice (my bet
        is a blue triangle or a Ulysses, butterflies down from
        Queensland)
   —so many blue flowers, fake and real
   —one of those miniature clothes pins, really two of them
   —a broken half crayon papered *cobalt*
   —that strip ripped from the space between cap and bottle
        and, of course, cap after cap after cap
   —toys, parts of toys: Legos, two blocks (one small, one big,
        very blue, natch)
   —swim goggles' blue foam, a navy babydoll hat, a chewed-up
        Grover
   —a snail shell, barely blue, in shards
   —the thin ribbon pulled to open a cellophane-like anything,
        maybe still on cigarette packs (*Ha! Like you know. You
        haven't smoked for fifty years!* said the Archangel)
   —that wee journal you miss, its soaked blue blurring out
        whatever you wrote, so much rain then into now, your no
        inkling in this life that

under trees in low scrub *your* treasure in that homage and lure front-
ing *his* love shack's two clumps of tall grass making a narrow space
for two birds and the deed, a wish and a lust, a little civilized privacy
please, a charming mad answer even with fires about to nightmare.

But why *why* a glorious blue in the first place, this come-hither to keep a world going I guess I am best not knowing.

* * *

Fabulous outrageous termite mounds
multiplied by thousands

upon thousands, shock then dumbfound
all over the outback. Six-foot
palaces, castles, great manor houses
settlers broke into, carved out

to fire up for bread.

But the Ancients before them put their
loved dead in there, all ritual

and heartbreak, waiting for

termites to forgive the intrusion, to seal up
the mounds again. It took—
I don't know how long but surely

a stitching, close work.

I won't say kindness but just the thought of
certain thoughts on auto-insect-do-gooder repeat is—

why not see gracious for gracious, no matter the species?

Such lordly spires for air and cooling and food.
Living underground, some with wings.

Really stupid, geez! the Archangel chortled way loud.
I mean, who flies dirt's dark and narrow?

Why wings at all if you live down there?

Those tiniest veils not nearly as nice as mine, he sang,
their hind wings backloaded, in disguise.

* * *

No word of the fires, I began the day
as a chat again—white fronted, orange, crimson
with a brush-tipped tongue
like the honeyeater with fruit, with nectar.

How birds of prey (owl, nightjar) have camouflage coats,
the army within narrowed to an old rage in me.

The emu got it right: the Dreamtime stories!
And the Australian Coat of Arms and the stamps, the body politic,
the original social media. Plus they kept drinking
from broken water pipes, bowing in thirst, if not homage.

No word of the fires, I *was* you, you birds I loved in glass cases
about to fake-fly or land on artist-eked trees
out of epoxy clay, wings tucked in at the nest or the bower, beaks
open to complain or attack, tail up or down,
white-throated, blue-faced, red-eyed, head cocked or
looking down, sideview, front view, a wagtail
or a babbler, a large dove in my spare time,
one solitary female brooding.

I became a lorikeet, a whistler, one claw forward,
one back. Doubled at the nest, I morphed into
two birds—so many ways to be
a next thing. I wondered where and why not
the brush bronzewing, my head crooked or looking up,
long-legged, in a hurry, taken aback, curious, bored, stuffed
with arsenic and cotton to be fully forever
a bird in that moment.

No word of the fires. Even here and after the fact, a world away
I swore it got darker. As for Pliny and his bestiary,
he wandered about Rome, his toga stuffed with birds
still alive though maybe I dreamt that, sleeping
as Vesuvius slept for so long.

I was as *everybird* as a whistling kite can be, posed
with my shredded rabbit. I went goshawk,

wings spread as Nixon's were, his hands on the globe
pre-election, Norman Rockwell snapping photos in a ruse
for the silly portrait the man really wanted.

No word from friends near the fires
so my favorite of birds, I still tell myself,
is the osprey I should have been while the fish I stood on
leaked blood like the real thing.
You can't just pass the time in these times
doing nothing.

No lack of drama in that dusty museum
as the rare white-eyed duck looked on.

* * *

I admit I succumbed and did
shrink the Archangel into a cockatoo for the diorama, not
to be nice really though yes, he'd been
lobbying forever. To teach him a lesson, I put him
next to the sweet hungry brush-tailed rock wallabies needing
carrots and giant squash we cut
at the Reserve where rangers wanted to save them: threatened,
only some eighty left in the world.

A *great* world regardless, said the Archangel, since—fact!—
wow, I've finally *become* a cockatoo! Tricked out eternal life
for this brief down-to-earth super noisy-unnatural
dazzling spin in the hay!

You mean sky. You have to savor loft and air, I told him,
and seeds and berries, you have
to have empathy. The cockatoo is a flock bird.

I was readjusting his distance from the ground like
certain poets write poems vis-à-vis
a glass case, how to suspend him with wire
from the drop ceiling I made to look
like a big storm coming.

Hard going. He flailed a bit, worried his spiffy, now official
sulfur crest might get wet in the wind-rattle.

But rain! That's good news, the Archangel proclaimed
like a trumpet hates its mute, and ditches it—not the hate,
the mute. These fires, this drought,
dried-up rivers, all that. See, he said, I know things.
I *feel* for the place now. It's bad here.

His wings too small for his body. His head
still enormous, wobbling.

This wobble's my thinking, he said twice.
That's my brilliance pouring out
though be careful, keep that to a minimum in what

you write. Maybe not humble but make me—
how about pious?

Check your fourth-grade holy card collection,
that little wooden box you've kept for decades—

Remember I'm in there as *guardian,* my wings
over a couple of kids scared to death to cross a bridge
that never never was. See? Clues have been given.

* * *

Emu, you still here?

Yes.

Emu, what about . . .

What "what about"? Don't you get it?
I'm forever up, down on that blood-pounded road,
my head, my long ribbon neck—
strewn like trash to wind or memory or myth.
You will never forget me because
I'll never forget me.

But what's your permanent address?

Certain flags. And the big deal national seal where
I'm bookended downwind of that roo
to hold the country upright.
And an honest-to-god constellation, if the Dreamtime
gets starry so I —
oh to lie down for real!

Sure, but isn't the . . . ?

> *Yes, a coin worth a dollar where I'm standing in trees.*
> *Every hand in Australia warm to me.*

* * *

So it is I lie sideways into sleep.
So it is I lower into stillness.

Music? Let's walk, I told my husband
in that tiny house near dawn in the gum grove.
And get our kangaroo fix against
whatever the day's calamity to come.

Morning after morning, repeat until
step and every step is
to see them again, see them, to see them . . .

A hope, wasn't it?
Calling down such luck.

BOOK FIVE

Someone Told Us Streetlights Kicked on

midafternoons, sky gone to ash, someone told us the pond no lon-
ger went silver in wind.

Someone told us *Eucalyptus melliodora* is *melleus* (honey) and *odora*
(sweet smelling) though nowhere in the house even under
such trees did it not reek of the grate.

John the Bird Whisperer: *that golf course saved this whole section of
city.* No leaf to leaf = nothing to burn. A stay against disaster,
I thought, not just men in outfits bending grass with sticks.

Halfway through the fires she wrote: *Read Facebook where poets
are leaving a trace.* I pictured charred crucial words, a burnt
screen.

Across an ocean and a continent to an op-ed, a photo, the roo mid-
leap in flames stilled by a click no one heard because fires roar,
the camera almost too hot to hold.

What passes for rescue is future: at least the coast will swamp as
Antarctica melts to put this out, someone said among
hundreds forced to the beach between fire and water.

* * *

Those makers of the bird book I loved
must be gods, I wanted to tell

the Indigenous Elder before he went home
to his bad back, his yogurt, his

brilliant insistence who was, who wasn't
in the Dreamtime, not that it's

getting handed on, he said half to himself.
(Not to me, such secrets, I thought. No way.)

It's his worry and reverence I still look through
for cockatoos or galahs flattened to

vivid 2-D in that book, ravens next to
fairy wrens done up in detail and gloss.

I lose myself to beauty, what lives in air,
flashes red and yellow in frozen ink

which will never unfreeze. It's not that
I don't know the difference, not like

the painted ones in the book don't
love their perfection or will ever

understand the wind-worn real ones
that hunt and get hunted to doom

beyond these pages. (A mirror
looms up, after all, to reverse a face.

We'll never know what we really look like.)
That bird stood on a branch

like this? At water's edge? And flew
at an angle up or down? we will ask

and think the book knows bigger than life
pretty much, sure, the way shallow knows

profound in spite of itself.   I swear these birds
were once, each god who made this book

will say—howbeit sad and at some stricken point—
to take back what seemed promised forever.

* * *

The crown-of-thorns starfish like
something off a holy card
creeps over for a taste of sweet coral's

every color on Earth under the sea.
Saint Crown-of-Thorns Starfish to you, it says.

So many want me dead. Here's the divers' clever drill—

vinegar injected stops my luminous breakfast.
Right. I go rigid, then kaput.
My "forever enemy" (gee thanks, Great-

Chain-of-Being), the triton snail also sits
on that jury of urgent-despicable ways to end me.

Thus the hate I hoard like a charm—

even for water those tritons wallow in. Divers
drop by drop *that* to herd
the gaggle of us for easy culling, the snails'

faintest scent shot through the drink until panic
drives me to those needles and cheap acids.

Oh I ache to be left alone to *my own devices* (okay,

I adore clichés) in these mountains and valleys
underwater warmed by human time and indifference
where I am *nocturnally inclined,*

my flamboyant spines of terror upright, off my twenty-one
Ferris-wheel arms to *iridesce* me purple by dusk.

(You like that? *Iridesce?* My new verbs shine!)

Toward supper too I creep and I creep (love that part, I'm fast),
then triumphantly open and lower my gut to grind up
those coral fluttering their hearts out. Yum.

My heart? There's nothing new in the world
but the oldest hungers. Only three questions I ever or anyone—

Can I eat it? Will it eat me? Can I have sex with it?

Quiz: How many hectares of your precious reef do I

masticate in thirty days? ("Masticate" = *chew, munch,
crunch,* Spell Check's down-home options!)

Check me out, idiots: https://www.aims.gov.au/cots . . .
Then give it up—my reef, my reef, MY reef!

As for my own personal predator, those "protected" tritons—

going down, comrades! Their fabulous shells snatched
for cold cash. See? You can't kick out every one of me.
Native Species! I'm born bad to these parts,

merely oversexed, overeating,
over-making more of me, and more.

I'm grim. I'm beautiful. As the world.

* * *

The word *because* or how it backdrops isn't exactly
what that Elder ever
claimed to love,
           but the wanting at the heart of

every want, this seeing
the Dreamtime flow, change course, drought up, stop at
who-damned-the-river.
                Oh crucial

terrifying eternal spots blotted out where
the winding water now
hits land out of reach to the very people . . .
Where women
gave birth for so long, daughters and sons
come to the world in the blessed shade of impeccable
certain trees marked sacred for passage
in the Dreaming.

The outback. I hear it again: *Blood all over
 the earth out there.* That was
the Indigenous artist in Canberra as she walked
in black leather to her DR650

and stood in winter sun
              like an axis.

* * *

Four ways to remember the koala—

1) It never was a bear.

2) It slept twenty-three hours a day in the tops of trees.

3) And children said: when does it pee?
   And grown-ups said: when does it, you know . . .

4) It was never not endearing.

The nerve of you humans thinking how I thought. Or if I thought!
Such a load of . . .

Who are you to write my elegy? The Indigenous Elder was right.

Let it be known
I peed via dream. And dreamed
        a future when
                        another came close—

How dare you know my root.
Don't look at me, monster, how

I came to be.

* * *

With another's skin on the wound, so much
can be grafted though mostly my own hip or back will do.
If it's really the body and not metaphor,
some expert in cellular smarts could link-up those capillaries
like the guy on a chair at the basement power box
knows which wires, how and why
the fridge will work again, and the stove,
and the lights when windows darken. The windows

did go dark. And I took my friend's graft as gift: pictures
of the fire from her deck in Australia, sheet
after sheet of solid flaming red and black, sky
never like this to the south, her sickened pause for
photos to archive, to document, as people say,
rounding up the sum total, distance it for some point
called future: *this nightmare really happened.*

To frame and caption means the bloody bit might heal
in six weeks, a few years, a decade. A patient
opens her eyes post-surgery. Didn't she just lie down
minutes ago after chatting with the doctor, his
last vacation to some island she never heard of?
She feigned interest. Now she's here in this
cold room with parts of her missing.

I still imagine my friend sleeping. Trying to sleep. Fire
is a monster. No plot or plan, it never *intends.* So many creatures
in the bush or the city are shy and have no idea.
I don't want to say which ones, even now. I want to hide them.
But it's those who rarely make a sound that kept screaming.

* * *

Out there for the famous balloons,
the colorful sort that go up with little baskets of
people under, but we got the day wrong
or the time.

By accident then, because we heard it first,
a gaggle at sunrise, a cheeping, a gurgling—
was it birds? Put this

in a time capsule: autumn in Australia
and a god-awful racket, all those
trees in the way thus harder to see, dawn closer
to dusk than you realize.

Neither story, nor analogy. Not really
song either. Or a thought loved, handed down.

When people say *handed down*
it must mean more than stuff in the attic
for the next generation to throw out.

Those creatures. Gone chorus-high in the eucalyptus
next to Lake Burley Griffin. But that *handed down* must
include certain sounds made forever
and onward as long as
we don't burn up or sicken the world completely.

Was the Archangel among them? No, too self-absorbed
for that crowd though he *is* part bird as he
loved to keep saying. No mob of crows
it turned out, just the wily
misnamed *flying foxes.*
                    Bats! Bats in trees! Hundreds!

Landing? Coming or going?
We stood there, the way humans stand there unlike

Janus, Roman god of doorways stilled
this moment between wherever we came from
and some dream-drenched next.

Well, hunting all night is hard,
that god might have said, gazing hither and yon.

I saw from the ground
bats wrap themselves, each in a wing-shroud.
They hang there
as if eternally in wait on graveyard marble.
Still, their racket not a dirge.

To clarify: Janus got stamped to silver and bronze
for centuries, his head doubled in profile
to stare left *and* right, no way to stop

whatever future or install a take-your-pick past.

A coin Pliny must have fished out of his robe
looking down, thinking twice—both ways—and kept.

* * *

At pool's edge, the skinniest man alive, probably
the oldest I'll ever see. He takes a step to
the young therapist's cheer: *Let's boogie!* I expect her
to say *Pops* as in a movie from the '50s.

I expect a lot of things that never happen. Like a fall,
a crash to the floor if you have legs like that, two sticks,
a kid's drawing of legs—nothing, I suspect, he'd
ever predict for himself in the days of muscle and bravado.

I can tell you: feral goats get thin as that in the outback.
Or the sheep ghost-crowding the one sealed road that circles
half a continent and threads down past Uluru.
We'd come upon them stopped, to stop us though of course

we figured they figured we had nothing to do with their
craving plain water, pure and not so simple to find in drought.
They stared straight into us, into our impatience.
Our old impatience. What about that? So what about that.

* * *

Pliny. I almost believe what
he claimed about battles—
that it rained not fire but blood and milk, even wool.
Also straight from the sky, iron in the shape
of sponges, baked bricks, the sound
trumpets make, their sudden
out of nowhere—

Bestiary's dark
afloat first in the brain as

a wombat hit by a car, swollen
in weeds because death
is busy with its new commitments to
foul gases, to the tiny
break-down bacteria that take any flesh
and turn it to ether and earth.

Battle of climate or plague—
up there that wool
or milk. Imagine blood coming down again,
iron too, seemingly in the guise of
soft, a sea creature pleasured and adrift,

no great waters in sight, or scent.

* * *

Spirits released by fire and fear,
freed of their bodies to rise from ash and soot where
they dropped or were
caught by the burning groves,
koalas and kangaroos, ancient orders of wallabies,
skinks and lizards, the hidden wealth of nowhere-else
cherished mammals and reptiles, the perennial question mark
of platypus so weirdly bits-of-both plus bird . . .
As for the solitary wallaroos, they too out of their
flesh and blood in some kind of
between-world not like a dream or a bardo, not
like anything I could humanly tell you.

But their shapes must be gauzy and strange, a thought,
really a second thought circling
the charred toothy sticks that used to be trees,
circling slow, the way medieval artisans
took their time to cut into wood and ink up for
their bestiaries, liking to monster them a little,
add an extra leg or head to those
creatures, yet another scare to the other
grim wonders of their time
and time again. The hand goes looser and rogue
drawing a thing never seen though
the claims were real enough,
gone whimsical, cartoonish to us
who demand exactitude and always how many
left on the planet and why
oh why is that.

Our why falls from the sky in embers
to spot-fire any grassy place close, is lightning
that strikes from smoke disguised
as clouds over the no-rain bush or the city making
its own weather, is eucalyptus oil in the leaves
sparking the next tree to tree to tree.

Or it's secret and lethal as air = gas, our carbon,
our fault toward the long gone.

A poet in Canberra emails—*the poems*
should indeed be dark; so many animals . . .
At least three billion
into ash and charred bone or
who am I, and where? Numbed
hectare on hectare of blackened gum tree leaves,
ruined waterways.

I despair, a last sentence as she slipped off-screen.

Then to find it, from the Old French *despeare,*
that added *de*—an emphatic reversal
of *sperare,* "to hope."

Despair. The word has a history and I'm wrong,
no afterlife in it.

* * *

The heart is heavy but not with blood
or sorrow yet. It's the trouble gene five times
what it should weigh
as we walk around, pierced as hearts I remember
from school that showed up sweet
or gruesome on those bad art holy cards, bodies
split open, even the classic doe-eyed Christ
staring above little knives, little arrows flailing
every which way. His four chambers
if triaged—however sacred—straight to the hopeless
last third in Emergency's far corner.

Some perfectly resourceful creatures
don't have hearts. The stinging jellyfish, delicate
as a wedding veil or gauze the ambulance tech
winds round and round the wound,
has no heart. In the Great Barrier Reef, in real sponges too,
nada. The highest number (three!), what the octopus
needs to slip through an aquarium filter
down drainage, certain a great sea
at the end of it. The winner on land: once the huge
barosaurus fed his tiny brain with blood, eight hearts
to manage all the rush and lie-back,
working like the legislature of a small corrupt republic,
his world to be erased by a meteor.

For the koala, the heart must be
so unhurried. They sleep most of the day and night
high in eucalypts, trees with nutritious most
flammable leaves. I wasn't thinking *fire* then or *heart*
for that matter as I watched them be
a wonder up there. Heavy,
heaviest is retrospect.

* * *

Emu, is it true? An egg of yours
        morphed into the sun, is the sun.
Emu! That's crazy. Emu, who could even throw that far?
Emu, you listening?

Heard you heard you heard you heard you . . .

The quiet came back. A truck wheezed and roared.

The Dreamtime storied me!
If I lost a chick, I'd count and recount each back to the world's
very start. But that one, my little delinquent,
even as an egg.

Now that egg, that sun, blinds you, Emu,
dries out your blood in that ditch you were dragged—

Yes, where once all was water, where I knelt ten minutes a day to
drink with the others. I loved that
                                    like the animal in you
might love.

Afterword

Sleeping minutes or hours, animals must see each other repeatedly.

The youngest again, that orphaned wallaroo joey

out of his flannel pouch. His pensive look, his burrowing into me.

Because animals—don't we?—find animals in dreams all the time.

Where we tear each other apart. And run. Hide. Or come back

from the dead. There are signs in the woods to be dreamt—

a leaf turning, a stick breaks. Go back to a source.

(It's *the bush*, not *the woods*, an Australian said—or that Archangel.)

I sleep for another glance now, cockatoos as blinding white rags

in trees swinging upside down. Like I thought

fate for the longest time a kind

of reversal, not muscle or bones or beak but feathers

and sky, a way to look from a distance at

that branch down there. That one.

The raven's call I first mistook as *accident,* the pain

more remembered from dream than felt, say a child's hand

briefly caught in a grinder, a crying out

in the waking. An old sort of grinder

left behind in an opp shop

to be bought and treasured for when we're

back to zero at the end of time and one of us turns the crank to pre-digest something rumored once edible.

No, the bird's pause and repeat wasn't that. Not a shriek. A wail.

Was it early evening, a Friday,

 a whole week's *loud* outside about to implode?

Give way, said a road sign politely. Drink and Die, said another as if

Cheers! Toast the dark.

And in the desolate outback: Survive this Drive.

What of Pliny's *the world, is it finite?* before Pompeii got buried alive.

"It was just black . . . like driving through rain

but the rain was on fire" said a Canberra official in 2003,

#infernohowmanyandwherethistime in the museum display

of historic disastrous ends.

That joey really did wash his face like a cat. Then buried it in my arm,

my other hand on his head a little while.

Acknowledgments

Many. But to begin, all respect and gratitude to the original guardians of Australia, its Indigenous people and Elders past, present, and to come in the places I lived, walked, drove, observed, and loved in that remarkable country.

Then, foremost, my thanks to the Fulbright Program of the US government for my Senior Research Scholarship, 2019, to observe the astonishing wildlife of Australia, and to my host, the University of Canberra, especially the International Poetry Studies Institute, where my colleagues—poets Jen Webb, Paul Hetherington, Shane Strange; Indigenous (Barkindji) poet and novelist Paul Collis; and the institute's assistant, artist Katie Hayne—all do such wonderful work. Lasting gratitude to Karen Coleman and Thomas Dougherty of the Fulbright Australia Program and to fellow Fulbright Scholar Michael Socolow plus Connie McVey and their boys, Simon and Geo—such good company. Serious thanks to Ranger Karen Williams at the Tidbinbilla Nature Reserve, where my husband and I volunteered; to John Bundock, crack birder and photographer; and to Rudy Della—Flora, snake expert.

As for other Canberra poets and friends—Lizz Murphy, Sarah St. Vincent Welch, Hazel Hall, Geoff Page, Chris Dorman, Michelle Hetherington, Gwen Jamieson, and Dylan Jones—deepening thanks. Warmest gratitude to Elizabeth and Rodney Baxter, also in Canberra, who saved us. And to Melbourne poet Kevin Brophy and artist Andrea Lloyd for their kindness. For warmth, conversation, and the invitation to read my poems at the Winter School, the University of Adelaide's J.M. Coetzee Centre for Creative Practice in the Flinders Ranges at the Oratunga Homestead conference, my thanks to Centre director Jennifer Rutherford, scholar and writer of creative nonfiction, and novelist/poet Brian Castro. Thanks to the Museum and Art Gallery of the Northern Territory in Darwin for hosting my reading; to the University of Western Australia's ASAL "Dirt" conference community reading organizers, Toby Fitch and Claire Albrecht, who included me; and to other Perth poets Catherine Noske and Dennis Haskell. Ditto to New Zealand writer Diana Clarke for her wry thoughts.

To the marine biologists—Jonathan Barton at the Australian Institute of Marine Science in Townsville and those guiding us on and in the water via the ecotour company Wavelength out of Port Douglas—many thanks. In Sydney, to Miranda Samuels, Fulbright Scholar to the US; to the Australian Museum taxidermist, Katrina McCormick; and to Clare Willcox at the Art Gallery of New South Wales, earnest thanks. Also to kangaroo carer Susan Allen near Brisbane (and my sister-in-law, Katherine Worthing Boruch, who introduced us), to Damien Fegan of the Queensland Museum, and to Tabatha Plovits of Canberra's ACT Wildlife, where my husband and I volunteered to feed orphaned joeys. Thanks to Dr David Feudenberger, kangaroo researcher at the Climate Change Institute, Australian National University, for his instruction. And I remain grateful to the late sculptor Peter Rockwell, who in Rome, 2015, told me of his father's—Norman Rockwell—first glimpse of then presidential candidate Richard Nixon, who he was later to paint for *Time*'s famous cover (book 4, vii). Other sources to acknowledge: an image from the 1425 fresco by Masaccio in the Brancacci Chapel in Florence is here (book 3, iii); the quote in the poem "Afterword" is from an exhibit on bushfires in the National Museum of Australia; and book 2, iv opens with a passage adapted from the ACT Namadgi National Park website. Words of Pliny the Elder are from his *Natural History* (Harvard University Press, 1935).

Continuing thanks to the editors who took a chance on these pieces, most with independent titles, some in a slightly different form, in *American Poetry Review, Arts & Letters, Axon (Australia), The Canberra Times (Australia), The Cincinnati Review, Copper Nickel, Crazyhorse, The Fiddlehead (Canada), The Georgia Review, The Gettysburg Review, The Hampden-Sydney Review, Kenyon Review, The London Review of Books, The Massachusetts Review, Narrative, New England Review, One Art, Paris Review, Ploughshares, Plume, Poetry, Poetry London, The Poetry Review (UK), The Rumpus, Volt, West Branch, The Yale Review.* The lyrebird poem (book 4, v), first published in *New England Review,* was republished in *Poetry Daily.* For shelter and good company while early drafts of these poems were written, much appreciation to Yaddo and to MacDowell (where filmmakers Emily Vey Duke and Cooper Battersby, fellow residents, shared the phrase "bad baby" in another context, but it stuck with me to haunt and make trouble).

[88]

Immeasurable gratitude to David Dunlap, so much a part of all that went on in Australia—and everything before and since, for that matter—and to Will Dunlap, beloved presence and help in spite of great distances. Warm thoughts to Eleanor Wilner for her close take on this strange manuscript as it came together.

The elegy in book 3 is for Brigit Pegeen Kelly, dearest friend so deeply missed. The first line contains a sentence from her brilliant poem "Three Cows and the Moon," from *Song* (BOA editions, 1995).

Profound thanks to Australian artist/poet/composer Judith Nangala Crispin, a descendent of the Bpangerang and Gunnaikurnai people of the Murray River, for allowing on the cover of this book three panels of her heart-stopping *Four birds and a lizard return to their ancestors, on spider-strings, over Mt Cooroora in Kabi-Kabi Country*. A full list of all that makes up and happens in this work appears on the book's copyright page.

Finally—most crucially—an acknowledgment to and of every animal of that vast continent and reef I saw, wrote about, and no doubt often misunderstood, though always I was stopped and amazed: no words can express that amazement. Or my sorrow at the subsequent fires. That too lives in this book.

About the Author

Marianne Boruch's ten previous books of poetry include *The Anti-Grief; Eventually One Dreams the Real Thing; Cadaver, Speak; The Book of Hours* (all from Copper Canyon Press) and earlier collections from Oberlin College Press and Wesleyan University Press. Her work has appeared in *The New York Review of Books, Poetry, The New Yorker, The American Poetry Review, New England Review, Field, Ploughshares, The London Review of Books, Kenyon Review, The Rumpus, The Yale Review*, and elsewhere. Among her honors are the Kingsley-Tufts Poetry Award for *The Book of Hours*, the Eugene and Marilyn Glick Indiana Writers Award (national division), Pushcart prizes, inclusions in *Best American Poetry*, fellowships from the Guggenheim Foundation and the National Endowment for the Arts, and residencies at the Rockefeller Foundation's Bellagio Center, Djerassi, the Anderson Center (Red Wing, MN), Yaddo, and MacDowell. She was a Fulbright Professor at the University of Edinburgh in 2012 and a Senior Fulbright Research Scholar at the University of Canberra in Australia in 2019, which inspired this book of poems on that country's astonishing wildlife. Twice she's been a visiting artist at the American Academy in Rome and was named an artist-in-residence at two national parks, Denali and Isle Royale. In May 2018, she went rogue and emeritus after thirty-two years of teaching at Purdue University, where she established and directed the MFA program in creative writing. Boruch remains on the faculty at the low-residency graduate program for writers at Warren Wilson College, where she's taught since 1988. She and her husband live in West Lafayette, Indiana, where they raised their son. She continues her decades-long effort at learning birdsong, which is to say: *who* in the world is saying all that *what* out there. She also mucks about with watercolors.

Poetry is vital to language and living. Since 1972, Copper Canyon Press has published extraordinary poetry from around the world to engage the imaginations and intellects of readers, writers, booksellers, librarians, teachers, students, and donors.

Copper Canyon Press gratefully acknowledges the kindness, patronage, and generous support of Jean Marie Lee, whose love and passionate appreciation of poetry has provided an everlasting benefit to our publishing program.

WE ARE GRATEFUL FOR THE MAJOR SUPPORT PROVIDED BY:

THE PAUL G. ALLEN
FAMILY FOUNDATION

CULTURE

  | National Endowment for the Arts
arts.gov
ART WORKS.

A&
OFFICE OF ARTS & CULTURE
SEATTLE

WASHINGTON STATE
ARTS COMMISSION

TO LEARN MORE ABOUT UNDERWRITING
COPPER CANYON PRESS TITLES,
PLEASE CALL 360-385-4925 EXT. 103

WE ARE GRATEFUL FOR THE MAJOR SUPPORT PROVIDED BY:

Anonymous

Jill Baker and Jeffrey Bishop

Anne and Geoffrey Barker

In honor of Ida Bauer, Betsy
  Gifford, and Beverly Sachar

Donna and Matthew Bellew

Sarah Bird

Will Blythe

John Branch

Diana Broze

John R. Cahill

Sarah Cavanaugh

The Beatrice R. and Joseph A.
  Coleman Foundation

The Currie Family Fund

Stephanie Ellis-Smith and Douglas
  Smith

Austin Evans

Saramel Evans

Mimi Gardner Gates

Gull Industries Inc. on behalf of
  William True

The Trust of Warren A. Gummow

William R. Hearst, III

Carolyn and Robert Hedin

Bruce Kahn

Phil Kovacevich and Eric Wechsler

Lakeside Industries Inc. on behalf
  of Jeanne Marie Lee

Maureen Lee and Mark Busto

Peter Lewis and Johnna Turiano

Ellie Mathews and Carl Youngmann
  as The North Press

Larry Mawby and Lois Bahle

Hank and Liesel Meijer

Jack Nicholson

Gregg Orr

Petunia Charitable Fund and
  adviser Elizabeth Hebert

Suzanne Rapp and Mark Hamilton

Adam and Lynn Rauch

Emily and Dan Raymond

Joseph C. Roberts

Jill and Bill Ruckelshaus

Cynthia Sears

Kim and Jeff Seely

Joan F. Woods

Barbara and Charles Wright

Caleb Young as C. Young Creative

The dedicated interns and
  faithful volunteers of
  Copper Canyon Press

The Chinese character for poetry is made up
of two parts: "word" and "temple." It also serves
as pressmark for Copper Canyon Press.

This book is set in Athelas, a typeface
designed by Veronika Burian and Jose Scaglione.
Book design by Gopa&Ted2, Inc.
Printed on archival-quality paper.